Super EASY F( )D PRESERVING

Quick Techniques for Fresh, Fridge and Freezer Storage

Megan Cain

The Creative Vegetable Gardener

Happy preserving!
megan

Super Easy Food Preserving
Quick Techniques for Fresh, Fridge and Freezer Storage

ISBN 978-0-692-40880-3

First Edition

Published by Megan Cain, The Creative Vegetable Gardener - Madison, WI

Author: Megan Cain
Photos: Megan Cain, Amelia John Photography, Stocksy Images
Design: Rebecca Pollock

creativevegetablegardener.com

Contents

MY STORY

I Am the Lazy Food Preserver

When most people think about food preservation they imagine long hours toiling in the kitchen over a hot stove. That's not for me. I consider myself a lazy food preserver, if you believe in such a thing. I reluctantly can 1-2 batches of salsa each summer because it's difficult to imagine doing without it. But, besides that one day of salsa canning, the rest of my time is primarily focused on crops I can store quickly and easily. I like to put food away, but I don't want to spend my whole summer a slave to the task. I want to have time to enjoy the lazy, hazy days of summer in Madison - hiking, camping, barbecuing and festival-going.

I love to spend a lot of time with my garden, but I don't want to spend *all* of my time on gardening tasks.

So, over the years I have focused on what I call **super easy food preserving**. I am constantly on the hunt for ways to put food away with the **least amount of work possible**. I've had a lot of successes and failures and learned a lot about which methods are quick and easy. Sometimes things work out well and go on the keeper list (celery and kale), and some things get crossed off for the next year (frozen cauliflower – blech).

It's my pleasure to share what I've learned with you so that you, too, can become a lazy food preserver.

Happy Gardening,

Megan

Fresh, Fridge and Freezer Storage

Preserving food as close as possible to its natural state retains the color, flavor and nutrients. In this book we'll focus on the three quickest and easiest ways to fill your pantry for winter eating – fresh, fridge and freezer storage.

 = FRESH    = FRIDGE    = FREEZER    = DRIED

Fresh

Vegetables kept in their natural state in a cool, dry place in your house.

Favorite vegetables for fresh storage:

Garlic	Potatoes	Sweet Potatoes
Onions	Spinach	Winter Squash

A few herbs are best dried:

Marjoram	Oregano	Tarragon
Mint	Sage	Thyme

Fridge

Vegetables that can store for long periods of time with the aid of refrigeration.

Favorite vegetables for fridge storage:

Beets	Carrots	Leeks
Cabbage	Cucumber	

Freezer

Vegetables, fruits and herbs that are pre-processed
and best kept in a chest freezer.

All fruits	Collards	Peas
Basil	Corn	Peppers
Beans	Eggplant	Summer Squash
Broccoli	Garlic Scapes	Tomatoes
Celery	Kale	Tomatillos
Chard	Leeks	
Cilantro	Parsley	

WHAT THIS BOOK DOESN'T COVER

I have determined what I think are the easiest ways to preserve food using fresh, fridge and freezer storage. In this book I don't cover canning, drying, fermenting, pickling, salting or root cellaring. Each vegetable listing has a section titled *Other Ideas for Preserving* in which I often link to other recipes and ways to preserve.

HOW TO USE THIS BOOK

This book was created to mimic the style of a cookbook. You don't need to read the whole thing cover to cover. Simply go right to the vegetable, fruit or herb you'd like to preserve and follow the instructions.

AND FINALLY, BEFORE YOU DIG IN
A Word of Encouragement

Instead of making food preserving a dreaded chore, allow stocking your pantry to be a joyful challenge. Only take on what you have time for. Choose foods that will make you happy to dig out of the freezer or pantry during the off season. Give yourself permission to take short cuts and do whatever you need to do to get things in the fridge or freezer with as little pain as possible.

Even super easy food preserving requires a commitment of your time and energy. Celebrate yourself and whatever amount of food you put away for your family. Take a moment to pause and savor those homegrown tomatoes when you pull them out of the freezer to make pasta sauce in January.

Remember, a little food preserving is better than none…so shoot for that!

Preserve What You Eat

When deciding what to put away for the winter think first about what foods you actually eat throughout the year. In our house we cook from scratch several nights a week. Those dishes always start with tossing a generous amount of garlic and onions in the pan with some olive oil. That means we grow all of our own garlic and onions each season. We also eat a lot of beans and rice all year round so canning salsa and freezing peppers and corn are a top priority.

Take some time to answer the questions on the following worksheet to help you decide on your priorities for putting food away.

What fruits and vegetables do I buy from the grocery store on a weekly basis?

What meals and snacks are regular features of my family's diet?

Are there foods I want to eat out of season?

What foods taste noticeably better when I eat them during their local growing season?

Which foods provide the highest value when preserved? (What's expensive to purchase at the store out of season)?

What foods will make me happy to have stored in my pantry?

Below is a list of the fruits, vegetables and herbs featured in this book. Use your answers from the questions above to decide upon your top priorities for food preservation. Don't worry about *how* you will preserve them right now, just focus on what you'd like to put away.

Check your favorites:

Veggies

Beans	Cucumber	Potatoes
Beets	Eggplant	Spinach
Broccoli	Garlic	Summer Squash
Cabbage	Garlic Scapes	Sweet Potatoes
Carrots	Kale	Tomatoes
Celery	Leeks	Tomatillos
Chard	Onions	Winter Squash
Collards	Peas	
Corn	Peppers	

Herbs

Basil	Mint	Sage
Cilantro	Oregano	Tarragon
Marjoram	Parsley	Thyme

Fruits

Apples	Peaches	Rhubarb
Blueberries	Pears	Strawberries
Cherries	Plums	
Cranberries	Raspberries	

Shoot for Abundance with a Few Crops

If you are feeling overwhelmed with how much you want to preserve, consider focusing on putting away a lot of a few things. In my community garden plot each year I mainly grow four crops: onions, garlic, tomatoes and peppers. These four ingredients are featured in many of our meals throughout the year so they are the most important to put away. The rest of the garden space is filled in with a few fun to grow crops like basil, kale and carrots.

Take a look at the list above and narrow down your choices to your top 3-5 priorities.

My top 3-5 priorities for food preservation this year:

1.

2.

3.

4.

5.

YOU DON'T HAVE TO GROW EVERYTHING YOU PRESERVE

The name of this game is super easy food preserving. Whatever is the quickest and easiest way to get things into the pantry is the best way. Sometimes that means simply purchasing something you want to put away instead of growing it yourself. In my garden I don't have room for strawberries, winter squash or corn. These are all things I go to other farms for instead of my own yard. My yearly trip to the u-pick strawberry farm is a fun tradition and in a few hours I pick all of the strawberries I need for the whole year. In October I take a crate to the farmers market and fill it up with acorn and winter squash to use for the next six months. When you buy at the height of the season you get great prices and wonderfully tasting produce with the added bonus of not having to tend to the plants yourself.

SAVE TIME - KEEP RECORDS

Super easy food preserving means not having to re-invent the wheel year after year. Keeping records is the best way to accomplish this. My record keeping system for my garden is simple. I have a binder where I keep all of my garden maps, seed starting records and pantry records. When I am making pesto for freezing on a Saturday afternoon I check last year's record to see how many I put away. I'll think about whether that was enough or not and adjust the number accordingly.

Putting away more food that you use each year is a complete waste of time and energy. The goal is to put away exactly what we eat, nothing more. It's good practice to eat through all of your storage each year because the quality degrades over time.

Find my easy to use record keeping template at the end of this book. To print out more copies of the template visit my website at *creativevegetablegardener.com/ preserving-book*

RECIPE LINKS

When you see a recipe you like and want to find out more about it, Google the website and recipe name and it should show up in the search results. The digital version of this book has live links to all of the recipes. As an owner of the print book you can purchase the digital copy for a reduced rate at *creativevegetablegardener. com/preserving-book*

Food Preservation Supplies Needed

Super easy food preserving means you should be able to mostly use the supplies you already have in your kitchen. There may be some items that are worth investing in that will make the process easier, allow you to have a higher quality results and can be used for other cooking besides preserving.

PROCESSING EQUIPMENT

- **Bowls:** Large and Medium

- **Colander**

- **Compost Container**

- **Cookie Sheets:** Needed for spreading out some vegetables and fruits to pre-freeze them before moving them into containers. This prevents them from sticking together.

- **Cutting Board**

- **Food Processer:** Using a food processor to chop and mix often saves a lot of time. I use mine all year round for many kitchen tasks.

- **Funnel:** A wide mouth funnel makes filling jars easier.

- **Ice Cube Trays:** You'll need some ice cubes on hand for cooling down steaming veggies.

- **Knives**

- **Large Stock Pot:** Good for steaming and blanching.

- **Steamer:** Many stock pots have a steamer basket that fits into the pot and allows you to put the lid on.

- **Salad Spinner:** Great way to dry vegetables quickly after steaming and cooling.

- **Sink with Cold Water:** Needed to stop the vegetable cooking process immediately.

- **Towels:** Needed to lay out vegetables to dry or to use to pat dry.

- **Various Vegetable and Fruit Specific Gadgets:** Strawberry hullers, apple peelers, cherry pitters and other doo-dads are specific to certain vegetables. They are not necessary, but are sometimes useful (and fun!) to have depending on the volume of the crop you are processing.

STORAGE EQUIPMENT

- **Chest Freezer:** If you are going to focus on freezing food you'll want to invest in a chest freezer. Your home freezer has a defrost cycle that will prevent you from storing frozen food for long amounts of time without it degrading in quality. Our household of two people has a 7 cubic ft. sized freezer that we fill up and eat through each season. If I had to do it over again I would buy two small freezers so that when one is emptied I could unplug it. It's best to buy a new or nearly new freezer because old freezers use a lot of energy.

- **Cool, Dry Place:** If you want to store fresh food, it's best to do it in a cool and dry area. This could be your basement, a cold corner of your guest room closet, or a drafty area in your house. You do not need a root cellar to successfully store vegetables for long amounts of time.

- **Containers:** Glass jars, plastic yogurt containers, and tupperware all work well in the freezer. Be careful when storing liquid in glass jars, they are prone to breaking in the freezer. I store liquid in plastic yogurt containers and loose items like broccoli and berries in glass jars.

- **Freezer bags:** Quart freezer bags are great for storing usable amounts of vegetables and fruits. You can also store liquids in bags.

- **Crates or boxes:** When storing fresh items like onions and garlic they need to be in breathable containers like crates or cardboard boxes.

- **Sharpie Marker:** Label everything with the date and item before putting it into the freezer.

Some Quick Tips for Preserving Food

- Don't overcook the vegetables when pre-processing or they will become mushy and unappetizing.

- After the required pre-cooking time transfer hot vegetables to ice water to immediately stop the cooking.

- Spread vegetables and fruits on cookie sheets and put them in the freezer to pre-freeze before transferring to containers. This will ensure they don't stick together in one big lump.

- Store food in smaller containers in the chest freezer so you are more likely to use the whole serving.

- Label everything you put away in your pantry with the date and name of food.

- Plan out your meals with what you have on hand. Search cooking websites or the internet for recipes featuring specific ingredients. (Some of my favorite websites are in the Resources section at the end of the book.)

- Process the food as quickly as possible after harvest. This will ensure you are preserving it at peak flavor and nutrients.

- The goal is to eat through your whole pantry each year. Only put away what you will eat!

- Have fun and enjoy the process – it's a privilege to be able to store the bounty.

Veggies

Beans

You can save a little taste of summer by freezing a portion of your green bean crop.

Favorite Varieties for Storage:
Maxibel, Dragon Tongue.

When to Harvest: Harvest beans when they are slightly immature.

Prep Materials Needed: Knife, cutting board.

Best Storage Containers: Jars or freezer bags.

EASY STORAGE DIRECTIONS:

Freezing Raw Beans
1. Trim stem ends from beans.
2. Cut into smaller pieces if desired.
3. Pack into containers.

Freezing Steamed Beans
1. Trim stem ends from beans.
2. Cut into smaller pieces if desired.
3. Steam 1 lb. at a time for 4-6 minutes, until they turn bright green. Don't overcook!
4. Cool in ice water.
5. Spin in salad spinner or pat dry with a towel.
6. Pack into containers.

How Long It Will Last in Storage:
Raw beans – 6 months. Steamed beans – up to one year.

Other Ideas for Preserving:
Pickled Dilly Beans from *foodinjars.com*

Favorite Recipes:
Casseroles

Stews

Pot Pie or Shepherd's Pie

Beets

Fall harvested beets can be stored in the fridge for up to a year with no special preparation needed.

Favorite Varieties for Storage: Detroit Dark Red, Red Ace, Early Wonder.

When to Harvest: Beets pop up above the soil so you can decide how big you'd like them to be at harvest. Most beets are ready for harvest when the roots are 1/2 to 2 inches across. If you let them grow past maturity they become tough.

Fall harvest: You can leave your beets in the ground throughout the fall and harvest as you need them. But, you must get them out of the ground before it freezes or they will turn to mush in storage.

Prep Materials Needed: Garden clippers.

Best Storage Containers: Plastic handle bags with a few holes punched through them to let some of the moisture out of the bag. I usually double bag mine and put them in the back of the fridge.

EASY STORAGE DIRECTIONS:

1. Check for beets that have nicks or bruising. Put them aside to use right away.
2. Cut off tops, leaving about one inch of stem.
3. **Leave the soil on the beets.**
4. Make sure they are relatively dry. If they are wet then leave them out to dry for a few hours.
5. Pack into plastic bags and store them in your fridge.
6. Do not wash them until you are ready to use them.
7. Compost, freeze or save the greens for cooking. (If freezing follow the same directions as kale and chard.)

How Long Will It Last in Storage: Beets can last 6-12 months in the fridge.

Other Ideas for Preserving: Pickled beets from *foodinjars.com* are a popular canning item.

Additional Thoughts: Don't forget to keep the soil on for storage, this will help them last longer. I will often wash a bunch of beets at once in winter for use over the following few weeks. I put away 1-2 handle bags full of beets for the winter.

Favorite Recipes:
Beet Burgers, *Asparagus to Zucchini, 1st edition,* FairShare CSA Coalition

Basic Aioli for Burgers, *creativevegetablegardener.com/ preserving-book*

Megan's Root Bake, *creativevegetablegardener.com/ preserving-book*

Beet Packets with Balsamic Vinegar and Walnuts, *New Vegetarian Grill,* Andrea Chesman

Chocolate Beet Cake, *Edible Madison*

Broccoli

Home grown broccoli is more tender and tasty than store bought varieties. Growing a spring and fall crop of broccoli in the garden each season will provide you with plenty to freeze for winter.

Favorite Varieties for Storage:
Spring – Gypsy, Packman; Fall – Arcadia, Marathon.

When to Harvest: Harvest when the buds are tight and before they start to turn yellow and open up.

Prep Materials Needed: Cutting board, knife, steamer or stock pot, sink with cold water and ice, salad spinner, towels, cookie sheet.

Best Storage Containers: Quart freezer bags, plastic containers, glass jars.

EASY STORAGE DIRECTIONS:

1. It's common to find cabbage worms in broccoli. Soak your harvest in a bowl or sink full of salted water for 20 minutes. The worms will float to the top.
2. Chop broccoli and stems to desired size. (Yes, the stems are so tender, freeze them as well!)
3. Steam or blanche just until they turn bright green, 3-5 minutes. Do not over cook or they will become mushy. You want them to be al dente for freezing.
4. Immediately put broccoli into a sink filled with cold water and ice to stop the cooking.
5. Spin broccoli dry in a salad spinner or pat dry with towels.
6. Lay out on towels on the counter to dry a bit more.
7. Spread out on a cookie sheet and put in the freezer to start the freezing process.
8. After 1-2 hours transfer into containers.

How Long It Will Last in Storage: Up to one year.

Other Ideas for Preserving: Freezing is your best option.

Additional Thoughts: I usually put away 7-10 quarts of broccoli for use out of season. Broccoli can become over cooked very quickly when you are cooking with it. Add it to your recipe with just enough time for it to cook slightly.

Favorite Recipes:
Broccoli Basil Mac and Cheese,
101cookbooks.com

Vegetable Upside Down Cake,
Enchanted Broccoli Forest, Mollie
Katzen

Megan's Easy Pizza,
*creativevegetablegardener.com/
preserving-book*

Casseroles, Soups, Stir frys

Cabbage

Fall cabbage can stay in the garden until past the first frost and then move into your fridge for months of storage.

Favorite Varieties for Storage: Early Jersey Wakefield.

When to Harvest: Cut heads when they are full, firm and bright in color.

Prep Materials Needed: Harvest knife.

Best Storage Containers: Plastic bags.

EASY STORAGE DIRECTIONS:

1. Harvest by cutting the stem at the base of the head of cabbage with a sharp knife.
2. Peel off any bruised or brown outer leaves.
3. Pack in plastic bags and store in fridge.

How Long It Will Last in Storage:
5-6 months in the fridge. Pull off the outer leaves if they start to go bad in storage and use the internal part of the cabbage.

Other Ideas for Preserving:
Sauerkraut, *thekitchn.com*
Kimchi, *mynewroots.com*
Freezer Coleslaw, *food.com*

Frozen Raw, Chopped Cabbage:
Coarsely chop cabbage, pack in freezer bags, store in freezer 5-6 months.

Additional Thoughts: If I don't have room for fall cabbage in my garden I will buy heads from the farmers market in late fall to keep in my fridge for the winter.

Favorite Recipes:
I love mixing thinly sliced purple cabbage in with my spinach salad each night.

Rustic Cabbage Soup, *101cookbooks.com*

Savoy Cabbage Gratin, *Great Greens: Fresh, Flavorful and Innovative Recipes*, Georgeanne Brennan. I just use whatever green cabbage I have on hand for this recipe.

Carrots

A late crop of carrots is perfect for storing in the fridge for the off season. Carrots are wonderful eaten fresh or for use in your favorite winter recipes.

Favorite Varieties for Storage:
Bolero, Yellow Sun, Purple Haze – I plant a mixture of all three colors in my garden.

When to Harvest: You can usually see the top of the carrot poking out of the ground if you dig around gently with your finger. If you think they might be ready, harvest 1 or 2 to see how big they are. You don't have to harvest the whole bed at once. I usually harvest the bigger ones and let the small ones stay in there to continue to grow for a little while.

Fall Harvest: You can leave your carrots in the ground throughout the fall and harvest as you need them. But, you must get the carrots out of the ground before it freezes or they will turn to mush in storage.

Prep Materials Needed: Garden clippers.

Best Storage Containers: Plastic handle bags with a few holes punched through them to let some of the moisture out of the bag. I usually double bag mine and put them in the back of the fridge.

EASY STORAGE DIRECTIONS:

1. Check for carrots that have nicks or bruising. Put them aside to use right away.
2. Cut off tops.
3. **Leave the soil on the carrots.**
4. Make sure they are relatively dry. If they are wet leave them out to dry for a few hours.
5. Pack into plastic bags and store them in your fridge.
6. Do not wash until you are ready to use them.

How Long It Will Last in Storage: 6-8 months, sometimes more!

Other Ideas for Preserving:
Add to sauerkraut, *thekitchn.com*
Add to kimchi, *mynewroots.com*

Additional Thoughts: Don't forget to keep the soil on the carrots when storing. This will help them keep longer. I will often wash a bunch at once for use over the following few weeks. Carrots can store in the fridge until the next spring with no problem!

Favorite Recipes:
We eat a lot of our carrots fresh for snacks and with hummus.

Red Lentil and Carrot Soup with Coconut, *125 Best Vegetarian Slow Cooker Recipes*, Judith Finlayson. I just cook this on the stove, not in a crock pot. One of my all-time favorite recipes!

Vegetable Upside Down Cake, *Enchanted Broccoli Forest*, Mollie Katzen

Beet burgers with Aioli, *Asparagus to Zucchini, 1st edition*, FairShare CSA Coalition

Basic Aioli Recipe, *creativevegetablegardener.com/ preserving-book*

Megan's Root Bake, *creativevegetablegardener.com/ preserving-book*

Baked Carrot Oven Fries, *101cookbooks.com*

Celery

Celery is easy to grow in the garden and straightforward to freeze. Most garden grown celery is tougher than the grocery store varieties so best used for soups and stews.

Favorite Varieties for Storage: Tango.

When to Harvest: Cut outer stalks for fresh use throughout the season. When harvesting the whole plant use a knife to cut it out at soil level.

Prep Materials Needed: Knife, cutting board, containers.

Best Storage Containers: Freezer bags, glass jars, plastic containers.

EASY STORAGE DIRECTIONS:

1. Separate stalks and wash thoroughly in the sink.
2. Cut celery into desired sized pieces. (I like to slice it into ¼ inch pieces.)
3. Pack into containers and freeze.

How Long It Will Last in Storage: Up to 1 year.

Other Ideas for Preserving: Whole plant can be stored fresh in the fridge for several months.

Additional Thoughts: I usually grow 4-6 celery plants and put away 4-6 quart bags each season.

Favorite Recipes:
I use my frozen celery in any cooked recipe that calls for celery. It's not a good substitute for fresh celery because it has a tougher texture. It's a great addition to soups and stews.

Curried Butternut Soup, *Cooking Light Magazine*

Mushroom Sesame Tofu Stew, *Moosewood Restaurant Low Fat Favorites*, Moosewood Collective

Chard

Chard is planted in spring and will last in the garden until a hard frost. Freezing the leaves and stalks is the best way to keep it for winter use.

Favorite Varieties for Storage: Bright Lights

When to Harvest: You can begin harvesting the leaves of chard for salad as soon as they are an eatable size. Continue harvesting the biggest leaves throughout the season and the plant will produce until frost. Make sure to never harvest all of the leaves off the plant, leave some to help it photosynthesize and continue growing.

Prep Materials Needed: Cutting board, knife, steamer, ice water, salad spinner, towels.

Best Storage Containers: Quart freezer bags.

EASY STORAGE DIRECTIONS

Steamed Chard
1. Separate stems from greens. (It's best to cook them separately.)
2. Cut or rip leaves into bit sized pieces.
3. Steam or blanche for 2-3 minutes until wilted.
4. Immediately transfer to sink filled with cold water and ice.
5. Spin leaves in salad spinner to remove water. Spread out onto towels to air dry for 20 minutes or more.
6. Repeat same process with stems.
7. Now you can mix stems and leaves together for freezing.
8. Spread on cookie sheets and put in freezer for 30 minutes or more. When partially to fully frozen transfer to freezer bags.

Raw Chard: You can also freeze the leaves raw instead.
1. Rip or cut leaves and stems into bite size pieces and stuff into freezer bags if you don't mind them being one big chunk.
2. If you'd rather be able to separate them more easily, use the cookie sheet method to pre-freeze and then fill freezer bags.

How Long It Will Last in Storage: Up to 1 year.

Other Ideas for Preserving:
Pickled Chard Stems,
agardenerstable.com

Additional Thoughts: I am moving towards the raw freezing method because I haven't noticed much difference between steaming and freezing raw.

Favorite Recipes:
Quiche, my favorite quiche recipe is the Swiss Cheese and Mushroom Quiche from *Moosewood Cookbook*, Mollie Katzen.

See also kale and spinach recipes. I use frozen chard and kale in recipes that call for cooked spinach, *localkitchenblog.com/leafy-greens*

Almost Cheeseless Pasta Casserole, *101cookbooks.com*

Giant Chipotle White Beans, *101cookbooks.com*

Collards

Leave collards in the garden until after the first few frosts when they will become sweeter. Collards have a similar preserving process as chard and kale.

Favorite Varieties for Storage: Champion.

When to Harvest: Like chard and kale you can start harvesting the biggest leaves of collards when they are at an eatable size. Continue to harvest the biggest leaves throughout the season taking care to not harvest all of the leaves at one time so that the plant can continue to produce. Collards taste best after a few frosts have sweetened the leaves.

Prep Materials Needed: Cutting board, knife, steamer, ice water, salad spinner, towels.

Best Storage Containers: Quart freezer bags.

EASY STORAGE DIRECTIONS

Steamed Collards
1. Cut or rip leaves into bit sized pieces.
2. Steam or blanche for 2-3 minutes until wilted.
3. Immediately transfer to sink filled with cold water and ice.
4. Spin leaves in salad spinner to remove water. Spread out onto towels to air dry for 20 minutes or more.
5. Spread on cookie sheets and put in freezer for 30 minutes or more. When partially to fully frozen transfer to freezer bags.

Raw Collards: You can also freeze the leaves raw.
1. Rip or cut leaves into bite size pieces and stuff into freezer bags if you don't mind them being one big chunk.
2. If you'd rather be able to separate them more easily, use the cookie sheet method above to pre-freeze and then fill freezer bags.

How Long It Will Last in Storage: Up to 1 year.

Other Preserving Ideas: Freezing is your best option.

Additional Thoughts: I am moving towards the raw freezing method because I haven't noticed much difference between steaming and freezing raw.

Favorite Recipes:
Soups, stews, casseroles, quiches.

See also chard, kale and spinach
recipes. I use frozen collards, chard
and kale in recipes that call for cooked
spinach.

Leafy greens recipes,
localkitchenblog.com/leafy-greens

Corn

In my garden I don't have enough room to grow corn. So, a few times each summer I buy several dozen ears from an organic grower at my local farmers market and process them all at once.

Favorite Varieties for Storage: Any sweet corn.

When to Harvest: Two weeks after the corn begins tassling pull back the husks to check the kernals. Pierce a kernel with your fingernail, if a milky white substance emerges it's at peak ripeness.

Prep Materials Needed: Cutting board, serrated knife, stock pot with steamer, containers, sink or bowl with ice water, salad spinner, towels, cookie sheets, corn stripper (optional specialty tool).

Best Storage Containers: Quart freezer bags, jars, plastic containers.

EASY STORAGE DIRECTIONS:

1. Remove husks and silk.
2. Fill a pot with water and insert steamer. Steam corn until just short of done. I prick it with a fork and take it out when it's almost ready to eat.
3. Immediately transfer to sink with cold water and ice to stop the cooking.
4. Strip kernals from the cobs.
5. Pat kernals dry with a towel or put them in a salad spinner to take off excess water.
6. Spread kernals on a cookie sheet and put them into the freezer for no more than 24 hours.
7. When frozen transfer to containers. This will prevent them from turning into a block of corn!

Other Ideas for Preserving: I've read about people freezing the whole ear in its husk. I've never tried it but it sounds fun!

Additional Thoughts: Corn sugars start to turn to starch immediately after harvest. Process as soon as possible.

Favorite Recipes:
Vegetable Upside Down Cake, *Enchanted Broccoli Forest*, Mollie Katzen
Heather's Quinoa, *101cookbooks.com*
Megan's Beans and Rice, *creativevegetablegardener.com/ preserving-book*
Soups, Stews, Casseroles
Firecracker Cornbread, *101cookbooks.com*

Cucumbers

If you don't have energy or time for canning pickles you can make fresh refrigerator pickles instead.

Favorite Varieties for Storage: You can use slicing or pickling cucumbers for this fridge recipe.

When to Harvest: Pick the fruits frequently and before they get too large. The more you pick cucumbers the longer they'll produce. At what size to harvest depends upon the variety you are growing. Slicers are usually harvested at 6-8 inches and pickling varieties at 3-5 inches. Use scissors to cut fruit from the vine.

Prep Materials Needed: Cutting board, knife, vinegar, water, dill, salt, mustard seed, garlic, whole black peppercorns.

Best Storage Containers: Quart canning jars, old yogurt container, other plastic container or jar.

EASY STORAGE DIRECTIONS:

Refrigerator Pickles
- 2 empty jars
- 3 medium cucumbers
- 1 c vinegar
- 2 c water

- 1 T dill seed or fresh dill leaves and flowers from the garden
- 1 T salt
- 1 t whole mustard seed
- 1 garlic clove, minced
- 6 whole black peppercorns

1. Cut cucumbers lengthwise into desired sized spears.
2. Put cucumbers into a large bowl and sprinkle with salt and dill. Mix until evenly coated. Let sit for 30 minutes.
3. Put cucumbers into the jars. Add 3 peppercorns, ½ tsp. mustard seed and ½ of the minced garlic to each jar.
4. Mix together water and vinegar in a bowl. Pour half into each jar.
5. Taste brine and add more water or vinegar as desired.
6. Screw on lids and shake each jar to make sure everything is well mixed.
7. Store pickles in fridge. They taste better if you wait until the next day to eat them.
8. You can re-use the brine once or twice more. Once you eat all of the pickles refill the jar with new cucumbers.

How Long It Will Last in Storage: 2-3 weeks

Other Ideas for Preserving:
Spicy Quick Pickled Cucumbers, *foodinjars.com*

7 Day Pickles, *food52.com*

Additional Thoughts: You can use different vegetables to make all kinds of quick pickles – carrots, turnips, radishes, garlic scapes.

Favorite Recipes:
Quick Pickled Vegetables Over Herb-y Black Lentils, *happyolks.com*

Add them to your favorite potato salad for an extra punch!

Eggplant

The quickest way to store eggplant in the freezer is to roast it and scoop out the flesh. You can also make it into various recipes to freeze for winter eating.

Favorite Varieties for Storage: Asian eggplants like Orient Express, globe eggplants like Nadia.

When to Harvest: Pick eggplant when the skin is glossy. Press the fruit with your fingernail and if it doesn't spring back it's ready.

Prep Materials Needed: Cookie sheet, fork, spoon, oven, containers.

Best Storage Containers: Freezer bags, plastic containers.

EASY STORAGE DIRECTIONS:

1. Heat oven to 400 degrees.
2. Prick eggplants all over with a fork.
3. Spread out on a cookie sheet and roast until tender, 30 minutes or longer depending on the size of the fruit. You can check their progress by stick a fork or knife into the skin. Remove when very soft.
4. When the fruits have cooled scoop out the flesh and pack into containers.

How Long It Will Last in Storage: Up to 1 year.

Other Ideas for Preserving:
Make ratatouille, baba ghanouj, caponata or lasagna and freeze for winter dinners.

Pickled Eggplant, *foodinjars.com*

Eggplant "Meat" Balls, *communitygroundworks.org*

Garlic

Garlic is planted in October in most areas and harvested the next July. It's a low maintenance crop that stores for a long, long time.

Favorite Varieties for Storage: Any porcelain garlic is best for long term storage.

When to Harvest: When half to three quarters of the leaves have turned brown.

Prep Materials Needed: Hand clippers, twine, place to hang or spread garlic to cure, waxed boxes or crates.

Best Storage Containers: Waxed boxes or crates.

EASY STORAGE DIRECTIONS:

1. Garlic needs to be cured before being put into storage so that the paper around each clove dries out and can protect it.
2. Tie it in bundles of 10 and hang in a dry, dark place for 4-6 weeks. (Garage, barn, shed.)
3. After it cures, cut off the roots and stalks, leaving about 1 ½ of stalk above the bulb.
4. Store in boxes or crates in a cool, dark place. (I keep mine in the basement.)

How Long It Will Last in Storage: Porcelain garlic can last up to one year in storage.

Other Ideas for Preserving: When garlic starts to sprout in storage in winter you can prolong its life by chopping it and storing it in jars in the freezer. Read more about it at awaytogarden.com

Additional Thoughts: Garlic is perfect for the Year Round Veggie Challenge. It's definitely possible to grow all the garlic you'll need for the whole year. I plant around 220 in my garden. I save some for seed and eat the rest.

Favorite Recipes:
Use some of your stash to make basil pesto to freeze.

Roast whole heads to smear on bread with butter.

Use with your frozen tomatoes to make sauce.

See next page for garlic scapes.

Garlic Scapes

The garlic scape is the flower stalk of the garlic plant. It's best to cut them off so the plant focuses its energy on bulb production rather than flower production.

Favorite Varieties for Storage:
Hardneck varieties of garlic produce scapes, softneck varieties do not.

When to Harvest: In June in most climates the scapes will begin to grow up from the stem. The longer you leave them to grow on the plant the tougher and spicier they get. Cut the scapes with garden clippers.

Prep Materials Needed: Garden clippers, knife, cutting board, containers.

Best Storage Containers: Glass pint jars.

EASY STORAGE DIRECTIONS:

1. The easiest way to store garlic scapes for the winter is to make them into a pesto. See recipe below.

Garlic Scape Pesto
Bjorn Bergman
Makes 1 1/2 cups.

- 2 cups garlic scapes, roughly chopped
- ½ cup grated Wisconsin Parmesan cheese
- ½ cup walnuts
- Pinch of salt
- Pinch of black pepper
- ½-¾ cup Driftless Organics Sunflower Oil

1. Add garlic scapes, Parmesan, walnuts, salt, and black pepper to food processor and pulse until well blended.
2. Turn processor on and slowly add ½ cup oil. Once added, stop the processor and scrape sides to make sure all ingredients are incorporated.
3. Taste and adjust seasoning with salt and pepper.
4. If pesto is too thick, add more oil while processor is running.
5. Process pesto once more until it is creamy, about 1 minute.

How Long It Will Last in Storage:
1 year, possibly more.

Other Ideas for Preserving:
Pickled Garlic Scapes,
yougrowgirl.com

Additional Thoughts: If I have other herbs in the fridge that need to be used I will sometimes add cilantro, parsley or basil to the pesto.

Favorite Recipes:
Use pesto on sandwiches, breakfast sandwiches, pasta dishes and homemade pizza.

Kale

Kale grows in the garden from early spring through to the first hard frosts. It can be eaten fresh throughout the season and then frozen for easy out of season use.

Favorite Varieties for Storage: Red Russian, Lacinato, Dwarf Blue Curled Scotch.

When to Harvest: You can begin harvesting kale when the leaves are an edible size. Continue to harvest the largest leaves throughout the season taking care to leave enough leaves on the plant for it to continue to photosynthesize and grow more leaves.

Prep Materials Needed: Knife, cutting board.

Best Storage Containers: Quart freezer bags.

EASY STORAGE DIRECTIONS:

1. If you tend to have worms and insects in your kale it might be best to wash the leaves before processing.
2. Cut leaves from stems and chop into desired bite sized pieces.
3. If you don't mind them freezing into one big chunk simply pack the leaves into freezer bags.
4. If you'd like the leaves to be loose and easily broken apart, spread them on a cookie sheet and pre-freeze in the freezer for 60 minutes. Then pack into freezer bags.

How Long It Will Last in Storage: Up to 1 year.

Other Ideas for Preserving: Kale Pesto, *bonappetit.com*

Additional Thoughts: I substitute kale for frozen spinach in most recipes.

Favorite Recipes:
Megan's Joyous Kale, *creativevegetablegardener.com/ preserving-book*

Pan Fried Corona Beans and Kale, *101cookbooks.com*

Kale and Olive Oil Mashed Potatoes, *101cookbooks.com*

Add it to soups, stews and casseroles. See chard, collards and spinach pages for more recipes.

Leeks

Leeks can stay in the garden until the first hard frosts of the season. When nights get consistently frigid move them into the fridge or freezer for longer term storage.

Favorite Varieties for Storage: King Richard, Tadorna.

When to Harvest: Leeks are usually harvested in fall when they grow to full size. But, they can be harvested at any time when they reach a desirable size for eating.

Prep Materials Needed: Garden clippers, knife, cutting board.

Best Storage Containers: Plastic bag for fridge storage and quart freezer bags or glass jars for freezer storage.

EASY STORAGE DIRECTIONS:

Fridge Stored:
1. Clip off roots and trim leaves to about 6 inches long.
2. Store in a plastic bag in the fridge for up to 6 weeks.

Freezer Stored:
1. You are going to chop the white and light green parts of the leek.
2. Cut off roots and the darkest green part of the leaves. Dispose in compost.
3. Wash soil off the leeks in sink.
4. Chop leeks into desired size pieces.
5. If they are wet give them a spin in the salad spinner.
6. Optional: Mix with a little olive oil.
7. Pack into containers.

How Long It Will Last in Storage: Fridge – 4-6 weeks, Freezer – up to 1 year.

Other Ideas for Preserving: Make a batch of potato leek soup and freeze it for a late winter treat.

Additional Thoughts: Leaving leeks in your garden for as long as possible in the late fall will free up space in your fridge. Some varieties are hardy down to 15 degrees.

Favorite Recipes: Potato Leek Soup, *Enchanted Broccoli Forest*, Mollie Katzen

Leek Fritters, *awaytogarden.com*

Use in place of onions for a more mild flavor.

Onions

Onions are planted early in spring and harvested mid-summer. When stored in a cool place they can last until late winter or early spring.

Favorite Varieties for Storage:
Redwing, Ruby Ring, Copra. Look for storage onion varieties. You might have to start your own seeds.

When to Harvest: When the tops start to flop over this signals the end of the growing season for onions. You can use a rake or shovel to gently make the rest of the tops flop over as well. Then leave them in the garden for another 1-2 weeks to let the tops dry out and turn brown.

Prep Materials Needed: Garden clippers, a cool, dark place to cure the onions.

Best Storage Containers: Boxes, crates or anything that has a bit of air flow.

EASY STORAGE DIRECTIONS:

1. Onions need to be cured before they are put into storage. This will allow the outer layers to dry out and protect the onion.
2. Lay them out in a cool place out of direct sunlight. I spread mine out on old screen doors I lay across saw horses in my garage.
3. Once the outside skins are thoroughly dry you can clip off the tops and pack the onions into your storage containers.
4. Keep onions stored in a dark and cool place in your house.

How Long It Will Last in Storage:
6-9 months depending on variety and storage conditions.

Other Ideas for Preserving:
Some of the onions tend to sprout at various times in storage. In the fall I chop several quart bags of onions for freezing. In late spring when we have used all of our onions I move to my frozen supply. This allows me to go a full year with my own onions!

Sweet and Sour Pickled Red Onions, *foodinjars.com*

Additional Thoughts: I have stored my onions in my basement in crates for years. My basement is heated, but when we aren't using it I close the vents to keep it cooler down there. I grow 300-500 onions which we use for canning salsa and fresh eating throughout the winter. My onions usually last until sometime in April when the last of them sprout.

Favorite Recipes: We use onions and garlic as the base of all of our meals - first in the pan is some chopped onions and garlic. We especially like to use them when making pasta sauce and beans and rice.

Peas

Shell peas are the best varieties for freezing. Sugar and snow peas are better eaten fresh. In warmer climates peas often have a short season so freezing them for later use allows you to enjoy the harvest for more of the year.

Favorite Varieties for Storage: Green Arrow, Lincoln.

When to Harvest: When pods are plump and green. If you let them get overripe they will taste starchy instead of sweet.

Prep Materials Needed: Pot with water, sink with ice water, colander, salad spinner, towels.

Best Storage Containers: Quart freezer bags, jars or plastic containers.

EASY STORAGE DIRECTIONS:

1. Shell peas and blanch in boiling water for 1 ½ minutes.
2. Cool immediately in ice water.
3. Spin in salad spinner and lay out on towels for 20 minutes to air dry.
4. Spread out on cookie sheet and freeze for 30 minutes. Pack into freezer bags when frozen.

How Long It Will Last in Storage: Up to 1 year.

Other Ideas for Preserving: Peas don't translate well to canning, so freezing is the best way to save them for later use.

Additional Thoughts: Some farmers at my local market sell already shelled peas. If I don't have room for shell peas in my garden then I'll just wait until I see them at the market.

Favorite Recipes:
Vegetable Upside Down Cake, *Enchanted Broccoli Forrest*, Mollie Katzen

Wild Fried Rice, *101cookbooks.com* - I like to add peas and other spring vegetables to this recipe.

Peppers

If you choose the right pepper variety for your region you can harvest more red peppers than you can eat fresh each season. Peppers store great in the freezer for use all year round.

Favorite Varieties for Storage:
Sweet: Carmen, Jimmy Nardello;
Hot: Santa Fe Grande, Jalapeno

When to Harvest: You can eat and freeze green peppers, but red are so much tastier. Cut, don't pull, peppers from the plant. Harvest them all regardless of ripeness when a frost is predicted.

Prep Materials Needed: Cutting board, knife.

Best Storage Containers: Freezer bags or glass jars.

EASY STORAGE DIRECTIONS:

1. De-stem and de-seed peppers. (You can leave hot pepper seeds in if you want!)
2. Chop into desired bite sized pieces.
3. Peppers can be frozen raw so simply pack them into containers.
4. If the peppers are dry when frozen they shouldn't stick together. If you want to make sure they remain loose, spread on a cookie sheet for an hour in the freezer and then pack into containers.

How Long It Will Last in Storage: Up to 1 year.

Other Ideas for Preserving: Roasted Red Pepper Sauce, *communitygroundworks.org*

Pickled Jalapeno Peppers, *foodinjars.com*

Additional Thoughts: Frozen peppers don't taste quite the same as fresh peppers, so they are best used in cooked dishes.

Favorite Recipes: Vegetable Upside Down Cake, *Enchanted Broccoli Forest*, Mollie Katzen

Wild Fried Rice, *101cookbooks.com* - I like to add peppers and other vegetables to this recipe.

Potatoes

Potatoes are a staple of many summer gardens. They store fresh easily and will keep many months in a cool storage area.

Favorite Varieties for Storage: German Butterball, Purple Viking, Yellow Finn, Yukon Gold

When to Harvest: When plant is flowering that signals that the first young potatoes are ready to harvest. You can dig around in the soil near the plant and harvest the largest potatoes. Let the plant continue to grow until the plants turn yellow and die back. Then the whole crop is ready to be harvested.

Prep Materials Needed: Fork to dig potatoes, warm dry place to cure them.

Best Storage Containers: Boxes.

EASY STORAGE DIRECTIONS:

1. Dig potatoes being careful not to spear any of the tubers.
2. Separate any that have been pierced or damaged for immediate use.
3. Cure potatoes for 10-14 days in a dry, dark place.
4. Store in boxes in a cool, dark place.

How Long It Will Last in Storage: Longer at 35-40 degrees, shorter at 45-50 degrees.

Other Ideas for Preserving: Make a few batches of Potato Leek Soup to freeze for winter dinners.

Additional Thoughts: Light and warmth cause potatoes to sprout and turn green. If you have a small amount to store you can keep them in the fridge for a long time, sometimes until spring.

Favorite Recipes:
Roasted Delicata Squash Salad, *101cookbooks.com*

A Tasty Frittata, *101cookbooks.com*

Potato Leek Soup, *Enchanted Broccoli Forest*, Mollie Katzen

Kale and Olive Oil Mashed Potatoes, *101cookbooks.com*

Spinach

In northern climates you can harvest spinach in your garden up until the end of the year if planted at the right time in late summer.

Favorite Varieties for Storage: Bloomsdale.

Growing Tips: Spinach is extremely frost hardy and can withstand the coldest winter weather. In my garden, I plant it in mid-August and harvest spinach up until mid-December (sometimes even for Christmas dinner). At this time the spinach will stop growing because of low light levels. Mulch it with hay to protect it from winter burn and then remove the mulch when the weather begins to warm up in late winter (for me late March). The spinach will start to grow again and you'll be harvesting fresh salads from your garden in no time!

When to Harvest: When leaves are a desirable size for eating.

Prep Materials Needed: None.

Best Storage Containers: Spinach is best kept in the garden. It will survive the winter in the harshest of areas (zone 5b at my house).

EASY STORAGE DIRECTIONS:

Once harvested spinach keeps best in a loose plastic bag. Keep it on the dry side.

How Long it Will Last in Storage: 1-2 weeks in the fridge if kept loose and dry.

Other Ideas for Preserving: If necessary you can freeze your spinach raw or by steaming. See kale or chard section for directions.

Favorite Recipes:
We mostly eat our spinach fresh in salads.

Spinach Rice Gratin,
101cookbooks.com

See kale, chard and collard recipes for using cooked spinach.

Summer Squash

Most gardeners who grow summer squash end up with more than they need at some point. I find that I enjoy summer squash best when fresh during the summer. It tends to get soggy in the freezer, but can be used in baked goods, stews and soups.

Favorite Varieties for Storage: Any and all squash!

When to Harvest: Bigger is not better where squash are concerned. They can grow fast so should be monitored and picked daily. Keep the plant picked so it keeps producing.

Prep Materials Needed: Cutting board, knife, Vegetable shredder (I use my food processor attachment), colander.

Best Storage Containers: Freezer bags.

EASY STORAGE DIRECTIONS:

1. Shred squash.
2. Press into a colander to drain some of the liquid.
3. Pack into freezer bags.

Other Ideas for Preserving:
Quick Pickled Zucchini, *101cookbooks.com*

Make and freeze zucchini bread. Some great ideas at *foodinjars.com*

Freeze in chunks for casseroles. How To Preserve the Bounty, *davesgarden.com*

Favorite Recipes:
Zucchini Bread, *101cookbooks.com*

Zucchini Fritters, *bonappetit.com*

Add to baked goods, soups, and stews.

Sweet Potatoes

Sweet potatoes don't store as long as regular potatoes, but with the right temperatures you can eat them for a few months outside of the harvest season.

Favorite Varieties for Storage:
Georgia Jet, Beauregard.

When to Harvest: Sweet potatoes like a long, warm season to produce. Keep them in the ground as long as possible in northern gardens. Harvest right before or right after the first frost in fall.

Prep Materials Needed: Digging fork, cool dry place for curing.

Best Storage Containers: Crates or boxes.

EASY STORAGE DIRECTIONS:

1. After harvesting spread sweet potatoes in a warm, dry place to cure for 10-14 days.
2. After the curing process pack lightly into crates or boxes and move into a cool basement or room.

How Long It Will Last in Storage:
3-4 months or more depending on storage conditions. Ideal temperatures are 55-60 degrees.

Other Ideas for Preserving:
If your sweet potatoes are starting to spoil, cook them in the oven and freeze the cooked flesh for later use. Freeze some Sweet Potato Curry in a Hurry from *awaytogarden.com* for later.

Additional Thoughts: Sweet potatoes don't like as much humidity as regular potatoes. Don't store them in the fridge.

Favorite Recipes:
Sweet Potato Fries

Big Comfy Sweet Potato, *mynewroots.org*

Megan's Root Bake, *creativevegetablegardener.com/ preserving-book*

Tomatoes

Tomatoes are likely one of the most popular garden vegetables of all! A few plants will produce more than you can eat fresh. It's easy to put away enough tomato products so you never have to buy them from the grocery store again.

Favorite Varieties for Storage: Amish Paste, Speckled Roman, Green Zebra, Moonglow.

When to Harvest: The fruit should have some softness to it when pressed lightly. When ripe, tomatoes easily come off the vine when pulled. If you have to yank them off they are likely not quite ripe. Harvest the whole crop when frost is predicted.

Prep Materials Needed: Cutting board, knife, stock pot or steam table pan.

Best Storage Containers: Freezer bags, plastic containers, glass jars. Be careful with glass jars and tomatoes, they sometimes crack in the freezer because of the abundance of water.

EASY STORAGE DIRECTIONS:

There are a few ways you can freeze tomatoes.

Freezing Whole Raw Tomatoes:
(Quick, but takes up a lot of space.)

1. Pack whole tomatoes into quart or gallon freezer bags
2. Defrost before using.
3. The only reason I don't use this method is that it takes up too much space in my freezer.

Freezing Chopped Raw Tomatoes:
(Takes a little more time, but they won't take up as much room.)
1. Chop the tomatoes and drain off some of the water in a colander.
2. Pack them raw into containers for later use.

Freezing Chopped Cooked Tomatoes:
(This is my favorite method even though it takes a little more prep. It's the best way to fit the most tomatoes in your freezer.)
1. Chop tomatoes.
2. Put them into a stock pot or steam table pan* and cook them down to desired consistency. Mostly you are cooking off some of the water so that you are freezing more sauce than watery tomatoes. You don't need to add anything at this point, but sometimes I will put in some

chopped basil or other herbs I have from my garden. I have also added green beans and other vegetables.

3. Pack into containers and freeze.

*I use a steam table pan that fits over two burners at the same time. The tomatoes cook down much faster.

Other Ideas for Preserving:
Can or freeze Tomato Salsa

Five Ways to Preserve Large Tomatoes, *foodinjars.com*

Five Ways to Preserve Small Tomatoes, *foodinjars.com*

Freeze some Roasted Tomato Soup, *101cookbooks.com*

Additional Thoughts: There are so many tomato processing recipes on the internet. Take a look around and pick one that sounds fun!

Favorite Recipes:
Megan's Quick Pasta, *creativevegetablegardener.com/ preserving-book*

Red Lentil and Carrot Soup with Coconut, *125 Best Vegetarian Slow Cooker Recipes*, Judith Finlayson

When a recipe calls for canned tomatoes, use a container of your frozen plain tomatoes. I never buy canned tomato products anymore.

Tomatillos

Tomatillo plants produce such an abundance of fruit it is difficult to use it all fresh during the season. Freezing green salsa is a great way to save this taste of summer!

Favorite Varieties for Storage: Toma Verde.

When to Harvest: Pick when the fruit fills up the husk and it starts to separate. Make sure you harvest before they turn yellow as they start to lose flavor at that point.

Prep Materials Needed: Cutting board, knife, food processor and green salsa ingredients if needed.

Best Storage Containers: Plastic containers or jars (caution: if it's too watery the jars may break).

EASY STORAGE DIRECTIONS:

Raw Whole Fruits:
1. Remove their husks.
2. Make sure they're clean and pack them into containers.

Raw Chopped Fruits:
1. Chop whole fruits in a food processor to desired consistency.
2. Pack into containers and freeze.

Raw Green Salsa:
1. Assemble ingredients for green salsa from recipe linked below.
2. Pack into containers (might be too watery for glass) and freeze.
3. It has a bit of water when defrosted, so you might want to cook it down a little before using.

Cooked Green Salsa:
1. Assemble ingredients for green salsa from recipe linked below.
2. Raw frozen green salsa can be watery when defrosted. I like to cook mine down in a pot before freezing to remove some of the water.
3. Transfer salsa to a stock pot and cook until it's at your desired consistency.
4. Cool and pack into containers.

How Long It Will Last in Storage: Up to 1 year, maybe more.

Additional Thoughts: You need more than one tomatillo plant for pollination. Don't just plant one!

Favorite Recipes:
Enchiladas – use your green and red salsa to make fancy enchiladas.

Megan's Beans and Rice, *creativevegetablegardener.com/ preserving-book*

Fresh Tomatillo Salsa, *pinchmysalt.com*

Oven Roasted Salsa Verde, *yougrowgirl.com*

Winter Squash

You can eat winter squash for many months outside of the harvest season if you buy or grow storage varieties.

Favorite Varieties for Storage: Early Butternut, Acorn.

When to Harvest: Acorn is ready when the orange spot where it touches the ground is bright and vivid. Butternut will turn from a pale greenish tint to a more brown/tan color. Ripe squashes should resist a light press of your fingernail. Make sure you get them out of the garden before the first frost.

Prep Materials Needed: Garden clippers, place to cure squash.

Best Storage Containers: Crates or boxes.

EASY STORAGE DIRECTIONS:

1. Set squash in a warm, dark place for about a week after harvest to cure.
2. Inspect for damage. Any squash that have bruises or nicks should be used first.
3. Set in crates or boxes and store in a cool, dry place. I store mine in my basement.
4. Acorn squash should be used first because it keeps for a shorter time than butternut.
5. Periodically check on squash during the winter to make sure it's not spoiling.

How Long It Will Last in Storage: Acorn squash lasts 2-3 months, butternut squash 6-8 months.

Other Ideas for Preserving: Roast the squash and scrape out the flesh. Pack into containers and freeze.

Additional Thoughts: I don't grow my own winter squash because I don't have room in my garden. In the fall I take a trip to my local farmers market and load up a few boxes with the amount of squash I think I'll need for the winter. It's much less expensive to buy butternut squash in the height of the season than in the middle of winter when it comes from far away.

Favorite Recipes:
Butternut Squash and Parsnip Pasta, *cookinglight.com*

Curried Butternut Soup, *Cooking Light Magazine*

Roasted Corn Pudding in Acorn Squash, *101cookbooks.com*

Roasted Pumpkin Salad,
101cookbooks.com - I use squash
instead of pumpkin for this recipe.

SUPER EASY FOOD PRESERVING

Herbs

Basil

Basil doesn't have much taste when dried. Your best bet is to freeze it fresh or in pesto. With one or two quick sessions you can make all of the pesto you'll need for a whole year.

Favorite Varieties for Storage: Genovese.

When to Harvest: Harvest basil before it goes to flower. Use clippers to cut the stalks from the top down. The plant likes to be cut back periodically and will regrow.

Prep Materials Needed: Garden clippers, pesto recipe with ingredients, food processor.

Best Storage Containers: Glass jam jars.

EASY STORAGE DIRECTIONS:

Basil Ice Cubes
1. Chop or julienne basil.
2. Spoon into ice cube trays.
3. Pour water over and freeze.
4. Transfer into containers when they are frozen.

Basil Pesto
1. Use your favorite pesto recipe to make a batch of pesto from *thekitchn.com*.
2. I use walnuts instead of pine nuts.
3. Transfer pesto into containers and freeze. I use glass jam jars.

How Long It Will Last in Storage: Up to 1 year.

Other Ideas for Preserving: Frozen cubes or pesto are the two best ways to preserve basil.

Additional Thoughts: Mix together several herbs into one pesto. Try the Five Herb Pesto from *101cookbooks.com*

Favorite Recipes:
Minestrone Genoa Soup, *Moosewood Restaurant Low Fat Favorites*, Moosewood Collective - great way to use up some pesto
Heather's Quinoa, *101cookbooks.com*
Megan's Easy Pizza, creativevegetablegardener.com/preserving-book

Use pesto in soups, stews, egg dishes, as a spread for crackers or bread.

Use basil ice cubes in soups, stews, tomato sauce.

Use your favorite pesto recipe or use the recipe from *thekitchn.com*.

Cilantro, Parsley

Cilantro and parsley lose a lot of their flavor when dried. Freezing them is quick, easy and will result in a tastier product.

Favorite Varieties for Storage:
Cilantro – Santo; Parsley – any flat leaf variety.

When to Harvest: Harvest cilantro before it goes to seed. Parsley can be harvested all season long. If it pushes up a flower stalk remove it with clippers.

Prep Materials Needed: Scissors, knife, cutting board, ice cube trays.

Best Storage Containers: Freezer bags.

EASY STORAGE DIRECTIONS:

Cilantro or Parsley Ice Cubes
1. Chop herb.
2. Spoon into ice cube trays.
3. Pour water over and freeze.
4. Transfer into containers when they are frozen.

Cilantro or Parsley Logs
1. My favorite method is from Grow and Storing a Year of Parsley at *awaytogarden.com*.

Other Ideas for Preserving: Use your favorite basil pesto recipe and mix in some cilantro and/or parsley.

Favorite Recipes:
Roasted Pumpkin Salad, *101cookbooks.com*

Green Curry Porridge, *101cookbooks.com*

Use in soups, stews, tabbouli, egg dishes, as a spread for crackers or bread.

Marjoram, Mint, Oregano, Sage, Tarragon, Thyme

All of these herbs can be dried and stored in jars for year round use. They taste much fresher than store bought herbs!

Favorite Varieties for Storage: Any variety you have in your garden will do.

When to Harvest: All of these herbs are best harvested before the plants flower.

Prep Materials Needed: Garden clippers, place to dry herbs.

Best Storage Containers: Glass spice jars.

EASY STORAGE DIRECTIONS:

Dried Herbs
1. Spread herbs in a dark, dry place to dry for several weeks. I use my cooling racks spread out in my laundry room which doesn't have a window.
2. Or, you can tie the herbs in bundles and hang them in a dark, dry place.
3. Check on them after a few weeks. You want the leaves to be so dry they are brittle and crush easily.
4. Use a big bowl and remove the leaves from the stems.
5. Transfer to spice jars and store in a cupboard in your kitchen.

How Long It Will Last in Storage: Less than 6 months.

Other Ideas for Preserving: Mix the fresh herbs into your favorite pesto recipe to add a slightly different flavor.

Favorite Recipes: I use my dried herbs in recipes all winter long.

Fruits & Berries

Blueberries, Cranberries, Raspberries, Rhubarb, Strawberries

All of these fruits can be frozen in their just picked state. It can't get easier than that!

Favorite Varieties for Storage: Any variety you have access to is great!

When to Harvest: All of these fruits are best harvested when they are at the peak of ripeness or slightly under ripe.

Prep Materials Needed: Trays or cookie sheets.

Best Storage Containers: Freezer bags or jars.

EASY STORAGE DIRECTIONS:

1. Prep fruit: Hull strawberries. Remove rhubarb stems from leaves and discard. Chop stems.
2. Wash and dry fruit if necessary.
3. Spread fruit on a cookie sheet. (Line with wax paper if you don't want them to stick.)
4. Leave to freeze for up to 24 hours.
5. Transfer into containers within a day or they will get freezer burn.

How Long It Will Last in Storage: Up to 1 year.

Other Ideas for Preserving: All of these fruits can be make into a quick freezer jam or sauce for freezing.

Additional Thoughts: Spending a day picking fruit at a nearby farm is a great way to get enough to freeze for a whole year's use.

Favorite Recipes:
Smoothies

Baked goods

Fruit Sauces

Apples, Peaches, Pears, Plums

Unlike berries, these fruits need a little bit of prep for freezing.

Favorite Varieties for Storage: Any variety you have access to is great!

When to Harvest: All of these fruits are best harvested when they are slightly under ripe so they aren't mushy when you are trying to preserve them.

Prep Materials Needed: Knife, cutting board, trays, ascorbic acid.

Best Storage Containers: Freezer bags or jars.

EASY STORAGE DIRECTIONS:

Apples, peaches and pears can turn brown in the freezer. If you don't want this to happen make sure you follow step #4.

1. Wash and dry fruit if necessary.
2. Remove pits of peaches and plums. Halve or slice into desired size for freezing.
3. Core pears and apples. Slice fruit into desired size for freezing. (A corer/slicer comes in handy for this task.)
4. Dissolve ½ teaspoon of ascorbic acid in 3 tablespoons water. Mix fruit in the solution to coat. Mix more if needed. (This is not necessary for plums.)
5. Spread fruit on a cookie sheet. (Line with wax paper if you don't want them to stick.)
6. Transfer into containers within 24 hours. Pack tightly and remove as much air as possible to prevent freezer burn.

How Long It Will Last in Storage: Up to 1 year.

Other Ideas for Preserving: To prevent browning and freezer burn you can pack fruit in sugar or fruit juice syrup. Read more about it in Farm Fresh Peaches Frozen to Perfection at *awaytogarden.com.*

Additional Thoughts: Spending a day picking fruit at a nearby farm is a great way to get enough to freeze for a whole year's use.

Favorite Recipes: Smoothies, Baked goods, Fruit Sauces

Cranberries ~ Mark Bittman's Autumn Millet Bake, *101cookbooks.com*

Cherries

Unlike other berries, cherries need a little bit of prep for freezing.

Favorite Varieties for Storage: I love North Star sour cherries. Any variety you have access to is great!

When to Harvest: These fruits are best harvested when they are slightly under ripe so they aren't mushy when you are trying to preserve them.

Prep Materials Needed: Knife, cherry pitter, ice cube trays.

Best Storage Containers: Freezer bags or jars.

EASY STORAGE DIRECTIONS:

Cherry Ice Cubes

The pitting of cherries mangles the fruit. It's difficult to freeze them whole at this point.

1. Wash and dry fruit if necessary.
2. Remove pits. (A hand held or free standing cherry pitter makes this job way easier!)
3. You'll end up with more of a cherry mash. I pack the mash into ice cube trays and freeze.
4. Transfer cubes into containers.

How Long It Will Last in Storage: Up to 1 year.

Other Ideas for Preserving:
Pickled Sweet Cherries, *foodinjars.com*

Lacto-Fermented Cherry Salsa, *nwedible.com*

Strawberry Jam Margaritas, *nwedible.com*

Additional Thoughts: Spending a day picking fruit at a nearby farm is a great way to get enough to freeze for a whole year's use.

Favorite Recipes:
Smoothies

Baked goods

Fruit Sauces

Tips for Cooking with Frozen Food

All frozen food is best used within a year as the quality and nutrients degrade over time. Aim to put away only what you will use each year by keeping records and tweaking the amount year to year as you get familiar with your eating patterns. Frozen food cooks fast because it is often pre-processed. Treat it differently than the raw equivalent of each vegetable. If you add it to the pan too early it may over-cook and become mushy. Add it to the recipe frozen so you have less chance of overcooking it. Monitor the frozen vegetables by testing them periodically as they are cooking. Basically you are just cooking it until it's hot all the way through; you don't need to cook it much.

Grow a Year's Worth Gardening Challenge

When I teach classes about Super Easy Food Preserving I like to pose a challenge to the participants at the end of class. I encourage them to pick one crop and try to grow all they will need for one year.

Pick something you eat a lot of; an item you buy at the grocery store each week. If you are a garlic lover, that's an easy one to start with. Garlic doesn't require much space or attention to grow and it's simple to store fresh in your basement. I plant 220 cloves each fall and that's plenty for our two person household to use all year and to save some for replanting each fall. Another easy option is tomatoes. With my frozen whole tomatoes and sauce I haven't bought a tomato product from the grocery store in many years. Pesto, winter squash, and beets are other possibilities. It's a deeply satisfying experience to provide yourself with all you need of a particular vegetable.

Garden Challenge!

I am going to attempt the amazing feat of providing my household

with all of our   **this year.**

COOKBOOKS & WEBSITES

The following cookbooks and websites are my favorites for planning vegetable focused meals:

- Asparagus to Zucchini, FairShare CSA Coalition
- *125 Best Vegetarian Slow Cooker Recipe*, Judith Finlayson
- *Moosewood Restaurant Low Fat Favorites*, Moosewood Collective
- *Enchanted Broccoli Forrest*, Mollie Katzen
- *The Moosewood Cookbook*, Mollie Katzen
- Heidi Swanson's wonderful website and cookbooks, *101cookbooks.com* - You can search by vegetable on her site.
- *My New Roots* Food Blog

My favorite gardening blogs:

- *awaytogarden.com*
- *foodinjars.com*
- *nwedible.com*
- *yougrowgirl.com*

For more reading on home food preservation:

- National Center for Home Food Preservation

RECIPES

I did not feel comfortable providing internet links to recipes when it wasn't clear whether the author had give their permission to use the recipe.

I've developed some of my own favorite recipes over the years. You can find them on my website, *creativevegetablegardener.com/preserving-book.*

Megan's Quick Pasta
Megan's Easy Pizza
Megan's Beans and Rice
Megan's Root Bake
Megan's Joyous Kale

My Top 10 Favorite Recipes Using Food From My Pantry

RECIPE	VEGETABLES USED					
Beet Burgers	Carrots	Beets				
Vegetable Upside Down Cake	Broccoli	Carrots	Corn	Onions	Peas	Peppers
Megan's Easy Pizza	Broccoli	Onions	Peppers	Pesto	Other veggies	
Savoy Cabbage Gratin	Cabbage	Onions				
Red Lentil and Carrot Soup with Coconut	Carrot	Garlic	Onions	Tomatoes		
Curried Butternut Soup	Butternut Squash	Celery	Garlic	Onions		
Beans and Rice	Corn	Garlic	Onions	Peppers	Tomatoes	Tomatillos
Joyous Kale	Broccoli	Garlic	Kale	Onions		
Wild Fried Rice	Broccoli	Garlic	Onions	Peas	Peppers	
Roasted Pumpkin Salad	Butternut Squash	Cilantro	Onions			

Year:

Fresh Storage

DATE	ITEM	AMOUNT	RECIPE SOURCE + NOTES

Fridge Storage

DATE	ITEM	AMOUNT	RECIPE SOURCE + NOTES

Year:

Freezer Storage

DATE	ITEM	AMOUNT	RECIPE SOURCE + NOTES

As an urban girl growing up in one of the largest cities in the U.S. I never touched a vegetable plant until the summer I turned 26. That's when I moved from my city life in San Francisco to a rural farm town of 100 people in Northeastern Missouri. After I got over the shock to my system I fell in love with gardening and the rest, as they say, is history!

I have spent the last 12 years of my life teaching hundreds of people of all ages how to get their hands dirty growing food in Madison, WI. I developed one of the early kids' gardening programs in Madison and a half acre youth farm. I have started my own home garden from a sad scrap of dirt and created an urban gardening class series that often has waiting lists. Through my business, The Creative Vegetable Gardener, I encourage and educate people how to successfully grow their own food and get the most from their vegetable gardens. My secret mission is to create a legion of gardening addicts.

KEEP IN TOUCH

Have a favorite recipe you want to share? Want to tell me about your successes with super easy food preserving? Have an even easier idea for a vegetable featured in this book?

I'd love to hear from you!

You can find me through my website at *creativevegetablegardener.com*.

Happy Gardening,

Megan